SCIENCE OF FUN STUFF

The Thrills and Chills of Amusement Parks

by Jordan D. Brown
illustrated by Mark Borgions

Ready-to-Read

Simon Spotlight
New York   London   Toronto   Sydney   New Delhi

SIMON SPOTLIGHT
An imprint of Simon & Schuster Children's Publishing Division
1230 Avenue of the Americas, New York, New York 10020
This Simon Spotlight edition September 2016
Text copyright © 2015 by Simon & Schuster, Inc.
Illustrations copyright © 2015 by Mark Borgions
All rights reserved, including the right of reproduction in whole or in part in any form.
SIMON SPOTLIGHT, READY-TO-READ, and colophon are registered trademarks of
Simon & Schuster, Inc.
For information about special discounts for bulk purchases, please contact Simon & Schuster Special Sales
at 1-866-506-1949 or business@simonandschuster.com.
The Simon & Schuster Speakers Bureau can bring authors to your live event. For more information or to
book an event, contact the Simon & Schuster Speakers Bureau at 1-866-248-3049 or visit our website at
www.simonspeakers.com.
Manufactured in China 0417 SDI

CONTENTS

CHAPTER 1
The Science of "Ahhhhhhh!"

Amusement parks have it all! They have thrill rides that make your heart race as you twist, turn, and get flipped upside down. And when you're ready for a snack, there's cotton candy, ice cream, and other goodies galore. Step right up and discover the science behind the rides you love and the treats you eat!

The wait is finally over! You stood in line for an hour, and now it's your turn to ride the roller coaster. Soon you hear *click, click, click* as your car climbs the steep hill. You scream as your car zooms down the track.

When it's over, you're dizzy but also curious. Why did you feel so light as your car zipped down the big hill? Why doesn't the roller coaster come off the track when it goes upside down? By the end of this book, you'll know the answers, and you'll be a Science of Fun Stuff Expert on amusement parks.

The Forces Behind the Fun

The people who create roller coasters are called engineers. Engineers are creative scientists who love coming up with ideas for interesting machines and then building them. When they create amusement park rides, they ask lots of questions and run experiments. In school, engineers learn about physics—the science of motion, energy, electricity, and much more.

One of the all-time great physics experts was Isaac Newton (1642–1727). Newton was a supersmart guy who lived in England more than three hundred years ago. Although he died long before roller coasters were invented, he probably would have loved them. After all, these rides bring many of Newton's famous ideas to life.

The Pulling Power of Gravity

In the 1600s, Newton used math and science to make some important discoveries. One of his big ideas was gravity. Gravity is the invisible force that pulls objects together. Newton didn't invent gravity, of course. But he figured out how gravity works. Newton explained that for very big objects, such as our planet, the force of gravity is stronger than it is for smaller objects, such as a baseball.

Gravity is why a roller coaster car doesn't need a motor to make it go. Once the car is pulled to the top of a hill, gravity does the rest of the work. When a coaster car zooms down the track, it works *with* gravity and goes faster. When a car travels upward on the track, it fights *against* gravity and slows down. By working with gravity, engineers make roller coasters exciting.

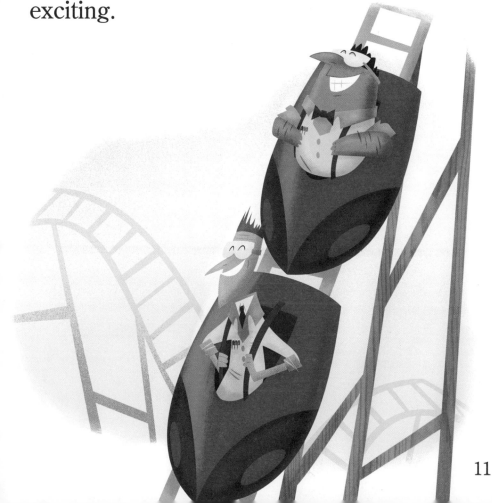

Laws That Coasters Obey

Newton wrote a book in the 1600s in which he described his three laws of motion. These laws help explain how roller coasters work. Newton's first law of motion tells us: <u>a moving object will keep moving—in the same direction, at the same speed—unless some force slows it down</u>.

A roller coaster car going down a hill keeps moving (pulled by gravity) on the tracks until something stops it or changes its direction. When the track starts to go upward, the car slows down (as it fights gravity). It's the sudden change in speed (called *acceleration*) that makes coasters so exciting. Newton's first law is sometimes called "the law of inertia."

Inertia is a fancy word for the idea that moving objects "like" to stay moving, and still objects "like" to stay put.

Roller coasters are fun to ride because they mess with your body's inertia. As your car races forward, your body wants to keep going in the same direction at the same speed. But when the car changes direction or speed, your body takes a moment to catch up with "the new plan."

The seat belt or harness pulls you back as your body moves forward. Newton's second law of motion tells us: <u>the speed of an object changes when an outside force acts on it</u>. And the heavier an object is, the more force you need to change its speed. This is why the tallest hill on a roller coaster is always at the start. To build up enough energy to move the car to the end of the ride, the car has to start on a tall hill. This helps gravity do its job.

Newton's third law of motion tells us: when one object pushes (or pulls) against a second object, the second object pushes (or pulls) back in the opposite direction. When a coaster goes through a loop, the car pushes on the track, and the track pushes back on the car. If the car is going fast enough, you'll travel all the way around the loop.

To help keep the ride safe, coaster loops aren't perfect circles. They are ovals (egg-shaped). This slows down your trip around, so you don't travel too fast.

CHAPTER 2
The Science of "Whoooaa!"

After riding the roller coaster, it's time for bumper cars. That's the awesome ride where you get to "floor it," spin like crazy, and even smash into other cars! Luckily, no one gets hurt. Bumper cars show physics in action. When the cars collide, Newton's laws come to life.

Imagine that your bumper car is perfectly still. Until a force is added, your car won't go anywhere, because of Newton's first law of motion (inertia). But if a car hits you from the front—*BAM!*—you go backward. That's an example of

Newton's third law, which says, "for every action, there is an equal and opposite reaction." The bump is the action, and your car pushing away is the *re*action.

All bumper cars in an amusement park ride are the same size, but the people who drive them aren't. Have you ever noticed that big drivers who get bumped move less than smaller drivers? That's because of Newton's second law of motion, which tells us that the bigger an object is, the more force is needed to move it.

Where do bumper cars get their power?
The secret is in the ceiling of the ride,
which has electricity running through
it. The long pole on the back of each car
touches the ceiling. When you step on the
pedal in the car, electricity flows from the
ceiling to your car's motor, and off you go.

Next up is the pirate ship—the huge boat that swings back and forth. As the ship swings near the top, you feel as if you weigh almost nothing. But when the boat swings downward, you feel extra heavy.

What's going on? It might seem like there's "different gravity," but that's not true. What you feel is the ride's swinging motion pushing *against* gravity or pulling *with* it. You feel lighter at the top because the ride is working against gravity and pushing your body up. And you feel heavier as you swing downward because the ride's force is pulling you down.

Some rides make your whole body spin. Take those big spinning rides where you stand up. You enter a round room with padded walls. The room slowly spins, and then goes faster and faster. When the floor drops down, your body sticks to the wall! Soon the floor rises to your feet and the spinning slows down. You're dizzy and dazzled. Why did you stick to the wall?

The force that pressed the wall against you is known as *centripetal* force. This force keeps a spinning object in a curved path. As the ride spun around, the wall's centripetal force tried to push your body toward the center. But your body didn't move! Why? Because it was pushing back with an equal, opposite force (Newton's third law of motion).

The free fall ride is like a roller coaster that goes only up and down. After you're strapped into your seat, you're lifted high above the ground. Then you suddenly drop, pulled down by gravity. During the drop you feel a gentle bump. You feel like an astronaut floating in space. What makes you feel weightless? The answer has to do with discoveries by the Italian scientist Galileo.

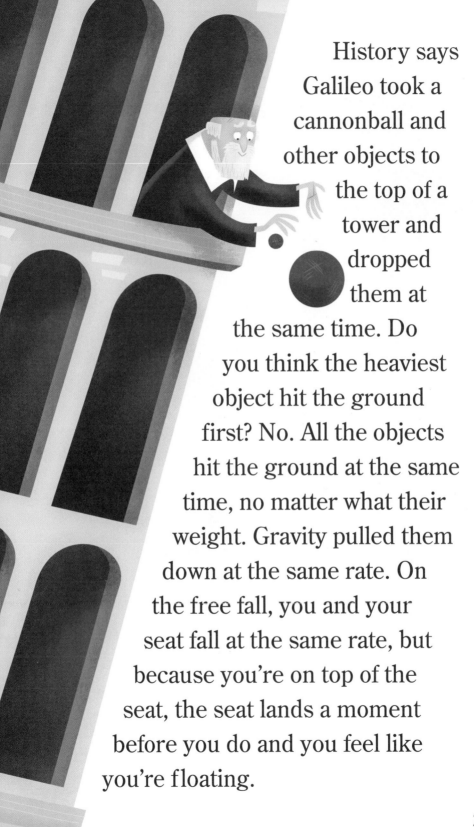

History says Galileo took a cannonball and other objects to the top of a tower and dropped them at the same time. Do you think the heaviest object hit the ground first? No. All the objects hit the ground at the same time, no matter what their weight. Gravity pulled them down at the same rate. On the free fall, you and your seat fall at the same rate, but because you're on top of the seat, the seat lands a moment before you do and you feel like you're floating.

Fun house mirrors let us see ourselves in weird ways. How do they work? Normal mirrors are flat, but fun house mirrors are bent. Convex mirrors are bent out and make you look shorter. Concave mirrors are bent in and make you look taller.

The secret has to do with the angle at which the beams of light hit your eyes. When you look into a concave mirror, you have to look up to see your eyes. But with convex mirrors you have to look down to get the right angle to see the reflection.

CHAPTER 3
The Science of "Yummmm!"

The science of how foods are created is called chemistry. Scientists study chemicals and explore how they change, or react, with each other. Cotton candy is a delicious example of chemistry.

Most of this sweet treat is made of sugar. Scientists call this sugar *sucrose*, and it is made of three things: carbon, oxygen, and hydrogen. When the sugar is poured into the cotton candy machine, the sugar heats up and melts. The heat breaks down the sucrose into its three parts. The hydrogen and oxygen combine to make water, and this *evaporates*, or disappears into the air.

What's left behind is hot, liquid carbon that spins so fast (sixty turns a second!) that it gets pushed out tiny holes into the body of the machine.

As soon as the thin strands hit the cool air, they become solid. A person then twirls a paper cone in circles to collect the fluff.

You know that feeling when you take a big bite of ice cream, or slurp an icy drink, and you get a horrible headache? Known as "brain freeze," this experience can be explained by science. Your brain doesn't actually freeze, of course. When you put a cold treat into your mouth, your brain senses the sudden change in temperature and thinks, *Whoa! Better warm things up.*

Your brain quickly opens blood vessels in your mouth and throat, and this causes blood to rush to your brain. This rush of blood causes the nearby nerves to give you a headache. But don't worry—usually brain freeze goes away in about thirty seconds.

CHAPTER 4
The Science of "Step Right Up!"

"Step right up! Win a *big* prize!" the guy at the booth shouts. All you have to do is win an "easy" game, such as knocking over bottles with a ball, or hitting a mark. Don't be fooled. These games are never as easy as they look.

That doesn't mean you shouldn't play them. But keep in mind that the chances of your winning a *big* prize are very small. To help your chances of winning, think about these games like a scientist.

Learn how the game is played and what helps some people win.

Ring the Bell—The goal is to hit a hammer onto a pad to make a metal ball go up a pole and ring a bell. You might think that strength is the most important thing. But aim is more important. You need to hit the center of the pad, with the hammer as flat as possible, so all the energy is concentrated in that spot.

Knock Down the Bottles—The goal of the game is to throw a softball at three milk bottles so that you knock them all off a box. But beware, some people make one of the bottom bottles heavier than the other two—so the ball doesn't have enough energy to knock it off. Then when the guy working the booth takes a turn, he secretly puts the heavy bottle on top. That's how he makes it look easy!

SCIENCE
OF FUN STUFF
EXPERT
on
AMUSEMENT
PARKS

Congratulations! You've come to the end of this book. You are now an official Science of Fun Stuff Expert on amusement parks. So the next time you go to an amusement park, remember the science behind the fun!

Hey, kids! Now that you're an expert on the science of amusement parks, turn the page to learn even more about it, and some world cultures, science, and amusement parks trivia along the way!

The History of Amusement Parks in America

Amusement parks first started in Europe in the 1500s and were originally called "pleasure gardens." The attractions included flower gardens, music, an area where people could dance, and a few simple rides.

Vauxhall Gardens was one of the first pleasure gardens to arrive in America. It opened in New York City in 1767. By the mid-1800s Vauxhall Gardens was also home to one of the first carousels in America. By 1875 another area opened up in New York that would eventually become a world-famous amusement park—Coney Island!

Coney Island was built by the shore in Brooklyn, New York, and as soon as a railroad was constructed in 1875 and people could get there easily, it became a very popular spot for day trips. At first, the area was known as a beach resort. But that all changed on July 4, 1895. That was the day Sea Lion Park opened at Coney Island.

It was the first outdoor amusement park in the world—a park enclosed by a fence with a fee charged at the gate. And Sea Lion Park's most exciting ride, the "Flip Flap Railroad," was the first looping roller coaster in America.

The Geography of Amusement Parks

The Coney Island amusement park was an immediate success. Soon amusement parks began popping up all over the United States. In 1955, a large amusement park opened on the West Coast, and people were flocking to Anaheim, California, to visit **Disneyland**. It was a winner, drawing nearly 3.8 million visitors in its first year.

In 1961 people began scrambling to the Southwest to visit the first **Six Flags Over Texas Amusement Park** in Arlington, Texas. It was an instant hit as well. In 1971 another major amusement park opened up in the southern United States—**Walt Disney World** opened in Orlando, Florida. Disney made the biggest investment ever for an amusement resort—more than $300 million.

In the 1970s many U.S. amusement parks were renovated to try to compete with Walt Disney World. They upgraded their equipment and added themed attractions.

Some examples are **Cedar Point** in Sandusky, Ohio, in the Midwest, and in the Northeast, **Dorney Park** in Allentown, Pennsylvania, and **Hersheypark** in Hershey, Pennsylvania. If you prefer your rides indoors, **Nickelodeon Universe** is based in the Mall of America in Bloomington, Minnesota. It is the largest indoor theme park in the U.S.

Check out the map below where we have marked the state for each of these amusement parks with a Ferris wheel. How many of them have you visited?

Amusement Parks
By the Numbers

Now that you know a lot about the science of amusement parks, plus a little about their history and geography, would you like to learn some fun math trivia facts about amusement parks? Keep reading!

The Tallest Roller Coaster

The **Kingda Ka** roller coaster at Six Flags Great Adventure in Jackson, New Jersey, is the world's tallest roller coaster at 456 feet high. Hold on to your hat and get ready for that first drop, it's 418 feet down!

Tallest Ferris Wheel

The High Roller is a giant Ferris Wheel located in Las Vegas, Nevada. It made its debut on March 31, 2014. At 550 feet up, it's the tallest Ferris Wheel in the world.

Cotton Candy—
A Sweet Hit from the Start!

In 1904, William Morrison and
John C. Wharton introduced
their cotton candy machine
to the St. Louis World's Fair.
The inventors sold cotton
candy for twenty-five cents a box.
It was a huge hit—68,655 boxes of cotton candy were
sold at the fair, so they made $17,163.75.

Tallest Flume Ride

A flume ride is an amusement park ride where
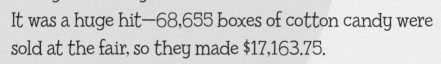
passengers float in a
loglike seat through a
narrow, water-filled
chute (a "flume") or
down a water slide.
The tallest flume
ride used to be the
Perilous Plunge
at Knott's Berry Farm in Buena Park, California. It
was a jaw-dropping 115 feet down. But this ride was
closed in 2012 because it was too dangerous. One of
the tallest flumes today is the **Jurassic Park River
Adventure** in Universal Orlando in Florida. It boasts a
scary 85-foot plunge!

Being an expert on something means you can get an awesome score on a quiz on that subject! Take this

SCIENCE OF AMUSEMENT PARKS QUIZ

to see how much you've learned.

1. People who create roller coasters are called

a. doctors　　　　　b. engineers　　　　　c. carpenters

2. The science of motion, energy. and electricity is called

a. physics　　　　　b. archeology　　　　　c. geology

3. Scientist Isaac Newton wrote a book describing three laws of

a. language　　　　　b. geometry　　　　　c. motion

4. A sudden change in speed is called

a. inertia　　　　　b. acceleration　　　　　c. response

5. Concave fun house mirrors make you look

a. taller　　　　　b. shorter　　　　　c. wider

6. Sucrose is made up of three ingredients: carbon, oxygen, and

a. salt　　　　　b. nitrogen　　　　　c. hydrogen

7. Gravity is

a. the weight of an object　　b. the invisible force that pulls objects together

c. a toxic gas

8. When water evaporates, it

a. gets heavier　　　　　b. disappears　　　　　c. freezes

9. You "stick to the wall" in a spinning ride because of

a. super glue　　　　　b. gravity　　　　　c. centripetal force

Answers: 1. b　2. a　3. c　4. b　5. a　6. c　7. b　8. b　9. c